D1733491

The Advent of Relationship

T.J. MacLeslie

The Advent of Relationship

Copyright © 2017 Peregrini Press. All rights reserved.

ISBN: 0993326579
ISBN-13: 978-0-9933265-7-8

No part of this book shall be reproduced or transmitted in any form or by any means, electronic or mechanical, including photocopying, recording, or by any information retrieval system without written permission of the publisher – except for brief quotations for the purpose of news, review or scholarship.

Published by Peregrini Press, a division of Awen Collaborative Limited

Cover design by Steppe Graphics
Web: http://po3aha.wixsite.com/steppegraphics
Faccbook: https://www.facebook.com/SteppeGraphics/

Interior nativity graphic by Rebecka Stewart

For inquiries related to this book please eMail :
info@peregrinipress.com
Tel : +44-(0)7597-170650

Scripture quotations are taken from the Holy Bible, New Living Translation, copyright © 1996, 2004, 2007 by Tyndale House Foundation. Used by permission of Tyndale House Publishers, Inc., Carol Stream, Illinois 60188. All rights reserved.

Every effort has been made to make this book as complete and as accurate as possible, but no warranty of fitness is implied. The information is provided on an 'as is' basis. The author and the publisher shall have neither liability nor responsibility to any person or entity with respect to any loss or damages arising from the information contained in this book.

DEDICATION

To the GOD who was, who is, and who is to come

CONTENTS

THE ADVENT –
AN INTRODUCTION

The term Advent comes to us from the Latin "Adventus" which literally means coming. The season of Advent is a traditional time of spiritual preparation, for the coming of Christmas and for the future coming of Christ. Christians have observed this special time of remembrance, preparation, and anticipation for more than 1500 years.

As we prepare to celebrate the fact that Christ came, so long ago, we reflect on the implications of the incarnation, the in-fleshing of God for us today. The fact that God became one of us, like a stranger on the bus, is one of the most profound mysteries of our faith, and is unique to Christianity.

Only Christianity tells this particular story. Other religions have men pursuing God and of God speaking, of God coming toward them; but only the Bible tells the story of the God of the universe becoming one of us. He did this so that we could become one with Him. It is all about relationship.

Over this Advent Season, I invite you to join me on a journey of reflection and anticipation, as we examine different facets of the beautiful jewel of the gift of God with us. It is dazzling from a distance, but let's not stay at a distance this year. Let's examine it carefully and prayerfully. Let's be amazed again as we stare into the depths of the mystery that lies at the heart of our faith.

This book was written with a heart for relationship with God and also with each other. While I hope it will be helpful for individuals, I have written it specifically for families and communities to experience together. That might include a daily gathering for reading, discussion, and possibly prayer, or it might be done individually with the idea of sharing the experience in community while only gathering occasionally during Advent.

Each day includes three items: 1 - An advent reflection to stimulate your thinking, 2- Suggested biblical passages that relate to the theme for the day, and 3- Some questions to help you reflect personally or corporately. I have tried to include questions that will help you to dig deeper, while also providing simple applicational questions that even young children can consider.

My prayer is that the words on the pages ahead will lead you deeper into the word of God and lead you closer to the Word that is God.

1 - THE ADVENT OF RECONCILIATION

Suggested Reading: Colossians 1:15-23

As Advent begins, I find myself reflecting on what it all means. What is the purpose of the coming of Christ? I have found a simple and potent explanation in the first chapter of Paul's letter to the Colossians. I am struck by the immensity of the miracle as well as by the purpose of the incarnation. God became one of us so that we could be reconciled to Him!

Have you ever been alienated from a loved one? Have you ever been estranged from a friend? Have you experienced separation where you desire connection, distance where you want closeness?

I have. I have experienced geographic distance, as I have lived across the sea from my family and friends. But I have also known what it is to be physically close but a million miles away in the heart. How many times have I looked across the table to a vacant look in their eyes? Physically present, but distant or guarded; not available, not here with me. We have all known broken or damaged relationships. We know the pain of it, but sometimes we do not know how to make it better. Sometimes we try, only to find our efforts at reconciliation rebuffed and we are left with more pain than before.

Relationship is the root and trunk of the universe. God designed and created us for life with Him. We are hard-wired for relationship. But we messed up. Both corporately and individually we have made mistakes (some of them wilful) that have broken our relationship with the Community that is our Trinitarian God.

So, The Trinity decided to achieve reconciliation where none seemed possible. The Son became one of us, a human being, while simultaneously also being part of the Godhead. He brought the two irreconcilable sides together in Himself. The God-Man reconciled God and Man!

Now, because of the miracle of the incarnation, we can walk and talk with God as Jesus did. This is the Gospel and the miracle of Christmas. Although once we were alienated, now we have been reconciled. When we could not close the distance, God broke through. Where once we 5could not reach Him, now He is with us! We never have to live apart from Him again.

May we continue to draw near and experience all that Advent means this Christmas, and every day.

....

Questions:

In what areas of your life are you aware of God's nearness?

How might you cultivate broader and deeper awareness of Him?

As you approach advent, is there anyone with whom you need to seek reconciliation?

2 - THE ADVENT OF HOPE

Suggested Reading: Luke 1:5-38

The world is messed up!

There are wars and rumours of wars. There are economic problems, political problems, racial problems, family problems, the list could go on and on. Proposed solutions and the people proposing them come and go, but the problems remain. In the midst of all of this, it is easy to become discouraged. Just a quick glance at the headlines on any given day gives us many reasons to despair and few reasons to hope.

We may imagine that we are living in a uniquely terrible time in history, but many generations have seen similar times and felt similar things. Empires have risen and crumbled and people in those times have lived through a level of pain and chaos that most of us have never experienced. And, I hope we never will. The Jews living in Palestine at the turn of the first century knew more about these things than we do in the West at the beginning of the twenty-first century.

They were living under an oppressive foreign regime who installed a puppet king. They lived under military occupation, subject to brutal treatment and crushing taxation. They longed for someone to deliver them. They lived in anticipation that God would intervene and save them, setting them free. They dreamed of the coming of the Messiah, the promised deliverer, the long delayed fulfilment of the ancient prophecies, already hundreds of years old in their day.

When Zechariah was ambushed by an angel of God in the temple, the plot began to thicken. There were rumblings and rumours – not of war – but of hope. Could this baby be the Messiah? Could this unborn child of a barren old woman and a dried up husband be the One? There were whispers in the hills of Judah. God is on the move! There is something special about this child!

But this baby, miraculous though his birth was, was not the One. There was another coming. A birth even more miraculous was on the way. Not one originating in the temple, but in a backwater town. God initiated another visitation, and another miraculous pregnancy, this time in a virgin womb. God's only Son became human, the Spirit of Christ enfleshed in the waiting womb of a willing young woman. Mary was to be the mother of Our Lord, the Hope of Nations.

The Advent of Christ was a rebirth of hope; more than that, a fulfilment of hope becoming flesh and dwelling among us. God drew near to us and demonstrated His love in the most tangible way possible, He became one of us. The God who created all things humbled Himself and became part of His creation. He began the remaking that will ultimately be fulfilled when His reign is fully established. But what a beginning He has made!

He is not distant or disengaged. He is not against us. He is one of us. He is among us. He is for us. We can know Him and know that He understands us. He is the reason for and the embodiment of our hope—the hope that came at Christmas!

....

Questions:

What pain, conflict, or problem is challenging your ability to live in hope?

How does the miracle of Christmas restore your hope?

3 - THE ADVENT OF INTERRUPTION

Suggested Reading: Matthew 1:18-25

Nobody expected God to come.

Sure, there were the old prophecies and the vague hope for a messiah someday, but no one was expecting God to break through and actively involve Himself in and through the lives of ordinary people.

Zechariah was minding his own business in the temple when he was interrupted by an angel. Even after the angel told him who he was and what was going to happen, Zechariah still incredulously asked for proof.

Mary wasn't expecting an angelic visitation, let alone a divine pregnancy. She neither asked for nor expected this invasive interruption of her plans or her body.

Joseph wasn't anticipating his virgin bride to fall pregnant until after the wedding. Upon discovering her unwelcome interruption, he immediately set about to do what any self-respecting, God-fearing man would do: break off the engagement with his shameful betrothed. Only another angelic visitation in his sleep convinced him to change his plans and adopt the Son of God as his own son.

The Magi were not sure what to expect as the stars told them a surprising tale of the King of the Jews to be born in a distant land. They stepped forward into their journey with an uninformed but sincere faith to see where the star might lead them; they prepared to worship the as yet unborn King wherever they might find him. The most obvious place to search was at the palace.

King Herod certainly wasn't expecting to have to deal with a new threat to his rule. He had effectively eliminated all who he perceived as a threat, not even sparing his own family. He was not expecting the inconvenience of a messiah, of The Messiah. The arrival of the magi was an interruption that he could do without.

The scribes and teachers of the law who told Herod where the messiah would be born, in lowly Bethlehem, were not expecting it to happen in their day. Even the arrival of the strange magi from the east and Herod's cryptic inquiry were not enough to pique their interest. They evidently couldn't be bothered to follow up on the lead they provided and went about their business, not terribly curious about an apparent messiah in their midst.

The shepherds certainly weren't expecting an angelic visitation, let alone an invasion with the armies of heaven appearing and breaking into song on that evening in the wilds of Judea. They were minding their own business, tending sheep, perhaps picking fleas from their cloaks or swapping stories around the fire, when they were terrified by the heavenly ambush.

No one was expecting God to interrupt their lives with good news of great joy. No one was expecting to be used by God to accomplish His marvellous purposes in history. At just the right time, although no one expected Him, and few welcomed Him, He came among us through the lives of ordinary people.

He does the same thing today.

....

Questions:

When has God interrupted your life or surprised you? What things limit your willingness to be interrupted by God today?

4 - THE ADVENT OF EMPTINESS

Suggested Reading: Philippians 2:1-11

I can't begin to count the times I've emptied my pockets before being allowed through security. It's a ritual of air travel now. Perhaps that's why I was so taken aback by a picture suddenly appearing to my mind's eye as I reflected on the miracle of Christmas.

I saw the eternal Son of God, the Christ, emptying His pockets. As I continued to ponder the image, I let myself imagine the conversation in heaven between the Father and the Son, just prior to the incarnation, and I watched as the scene unfolded in my mind.

The Father tenderly says, "It's time son."

The Son looks deep into the soul of the Father and says, "I know...I am ready to go. This is a good plan, and yet...I am afraid of what will happen on this trip."

"I understand my son. We have always been together, but for a little while it will be different. For a while you must lay aside all you have known and truly be one of them."

"Can I take my power? The power I used when we made the universe together."

"No my son, you must leave that here."

"Can I take my wisdom? The wisdom I have gained in our eternal relationship, the wisdom I have gained in the years I have watched our children upon the earth."

"No, you must leave that here. You will grow again in wisdom while you are there."

"Can I take my knowledge, the knowledge of all things from before the beginning of time?"

"No, you must learn. You must learn how to walk and how to speak."

"Can I take my glory that shines like the sun?"

"No, that too you must leave here."

"Can I take my all-sufficiency, my independence?"

"No. You will be entirely helpless. Not even be able to feed or clothe yourself. You will drink your first meal from a human breast and be utterly dependent upon your earthly parents. You must leave all these things behind."

"But how will I protect myself? We know how violent and unpredictable they can be! What if they try to kill me before our plan is complete?"

"You won't protect yourself. You will be utterly vulnerable. You will have to trust me. I will watch over you and no evil will harm you until the proper time."

"So, what do I take with me then? Can I take nothing from heaven to earth?"

"Just yourself. Only you, your essence, your Spirit poured into a frail human embryo in the womb of a teenage girl. You will start from there and show Us through one of them. You will show them Us, our Spirit, our Character, by living just as they do. You will be Emmanuel. You will be Us with them."

"Okay Father. I have emptied myself; I am ready...."

I don't pretend to know what happened in heaven, but I can only imagine.

Imagine what it must have been like for the perfect Son to contemplate leaving heaven. Imagine what it must have been like to empty Himself as He prepared to humble Himself and live in a human body. Imagine the miracle of the incarnation again this Christmas!

Can you imagine!?

....

Questions:

Are there things 'in your pocket' that you are clinging to?

What would you be willing to give up to help others?

5 - THE ADVENT OF POWER

Suggested Reading: Luke 2:8-15

As we draw near to Christmas, we often see nativity scenes and sing songs that reflect on little baby Jesus. There is nothing wrong with drawing up beside the manger and gazing in wonder at God wrapped in the skin of a helpless, human baby. It is good and right that we wonder at His humility and this miracle.

But there is another side to this story.

The miracle of the incarnation is a moment of incredible power. It was a decisive event in the destiny of the universe, the turning point of history.

When Christ emptied Himself of His divine power and knowledge, He performed a deed of breathtaking heroism. His submission in the incarnation was a heroic act of faith, and a dramatic step in the war in heaven.

The Apostle John was given a vision of what was happening on a cosmic level in the birth of Jesus. He records his vision in the 12th chapter of Revelation. John saw Satan, the enemy of God and of man, trying to prevent the birth of the Christ child and to destroy him, but God preserved the baby's life and Satan was defeated. Notice that he was defeated at the birth of the child.

The birth of Jesus was a military victory in the battle between good and evil.

Is it any wonder that when the angels ambushed those unsuspecting shepherds they were armed for battle?! Luke describes the shepherds as being scared by the appearance of one angel, but imagine their terror when the sky opened and they were suddenly confronted by a massive contingent of the heavenly army. One messenger angel was terrifying; I can't imagine the fear inspired by an angelic war host.

The Christmas story is not just about a humble carpenter and his virgin bride in a stable in Bethlehem. There is much more going on there than the simple surroundings would indicate. This is a momentous occasion of great cosmic importance. The armies of heaven were literally present in Bethlehem that night. Only the shepherds got to see them, but they were there.

The lonely couple far from home, giving birth to this little baby, and laying him in a feeding trough were playing their part in one of the most powerful and pivotal moments of all time.

I wonder what is going on right now. I wonder what God is doing around us and through us if we could only see it?

....

Questions:

Have you considered that you are part of a spiritual war?

What might your assignment be as one deployed on behalf of God's Kingdom?

6 - THE ADVENT OF GENEROSITY

Suggested Reading: Luke 11: 11-13

During Advent, some Christians celebrate the Feast of Saint Nicholas. Nicholas was a bishop and leader of the church in what is today Southern Turkey. He was known for his generosity as well as his participation at the Counsel of Nicaea. Nicholas gave generously and anonymously, sometimes throwing money through open windows, or down chimneys. From these devout roots grew the myth of Santa Claus. Behind the mythical generosity of Santa Claus, and the historical generosity of Saint Nicholas, is the immense generosity of God.

God is kind and generous to all His creation. He has created a beautiful world filled with good things for us to enjoy. Every good and perfect gift comes to us from the hand of the loving Father who created us and placed us here. The universe is an intricate and exquisite design with almost infinite diversity and power beyond our comprehension.

God gives us all we need to live. He provides the food we eat, the water we drink, and the very air we breathe; and He does this for everyone. He doesn't just give good gifts to those who love Him. His makes the rain fall on everyone. He generously gives to everyone, even those who will never acknowledge Him, let alone thank Him.

But there is a special gift that is offered to everyone, however not everyone receives. God offers Himself. He offers to buy us back from our wrong ways of thinking and behaving. He offers to free us from the slavery and tyranny into which we have sold ourselves. He offers redemption and freedom.

When I was growing up we had candy in our stockings, and small gifts under the tree, but there was almost always a big gift, an extravagant gift that would blow us away. We immediately attacked the candy in the stockings, and were always grateful for the small gifts, but Christmas was the one time in a year that my parents would give us a huge extravagant gift, usually beyond even our childish imaginations.

I can't imagine leaving the biggest and best gift unopened on Christmas morning? Can you?

God generously gives us all things, including Himself. He is the biggest gift!

....

Questions:

Are you daily receiving God's gift of Himself to you? How can you be generous to someone today?

7 - THE ADVENT OF PERSPECTIVE

Suggested Reading: Matthew 2: 1-12

I love optical illusions.

I particularly enjoy them when I'm not expecting them. I like that moment of wonder and surprise when you find that the picture you were studying is actually something else entirely, the flash of recognition when you suddenly see something that was there all along, but you failed to notice before.

The birth of Jesus was nothing of consequence from the perspective of the Roman Empire: just another Jewish boy born far from Rome, in an inconsequential corner of an unimportant province. Neither his mother, nor his father, was anyone important. He was just another boy born to Judean peasants who paid very little in taxes and who would never trouble the might of Rome. Little did Rome know that this baby boy would change everything!

The birth of Jesus was a perceived as a political threat to Herod. He saw a potential rival for the throne; someone whom his enemies could use to displace him. He feared the messiah would become a rallying point for the rabble, someone to lead them against him and his Roman allies. Little did Herod know that this little boy was no threat to his throne.

He wasn't born to assume political power or lead a violent insurrection. He was a revolutionary, but He was after men's souls not their thrones.

The birth of Jesus was announced in the stars to those who knew where to look. Astrologers from the East searching the stars for answers had seen something that caught their eye. They set out on a quest to see for themselves this thing they had traced on their charts. Having met the baby born in a stable, they fell down and worshipped this unlikely King. They recognized what others had missed. It's difficult to say how much they understood, but they laid their treasures at His feet.

Sometimes we miss Jesus. We may see Jesus and yet miss God incarnate. We can be staring right at Him and still not be seeing him.

It's a question of perspective.

....

Questions:

What things in your life daily direct your attention to Jesus?

What do you see when you look at Jesus?

How will you respond to Him today?

8 - THE ADVENT OF GROWTH

Suggested Reading: Luke 2: 39-52 and Hebrews 5:8-9

The miracle of Christmas is that God was born as a human. God became one of us, truly one of us. The Christ, the Son of God, became one of us as His body was formed in His mother's womb, just as my body was knit together in my mother's womb.

When Christ came to earth, He didn't appear full grown. Jesus was born into this world with the blood, sweat, and probably tears of His mother's labour. He was born as a baby, not knowing or being able to do much at all. He had a lot to learn.

Baby Jesus had to learn how to eat. He had to learn how to crawl, how to walk, how to run. He had to be potty trained. Jesus had to grow in knowledge and wisdom as well. It wasn't just physical growth. He had to learn how to relate. He had to learn language, or in His time and place, several languages. He would have learned Hebrew (the language of the scriptures), Aramaic (the language of the streets), and probably a smattering of Greek (the language of society and culture) and Latin (the language of government). He also learned a trade, carpentry.

Jesus didn't just pop into our world and start performing miracles. He lived a full life of childhood and through adolescence to manhood. In being born, growing, and learning as we all do, Jesus sanctified the process, He showed these to be holy activities, or at least that they could be done in a holy and sinless way.

I was struck by this anew recently as I was berating myself for failing to do something that I knew was best, that I ultimately wanted to do. I felt like I should be farther along already; I should be done growing. As I took this to the Lord in prayer, I felt the gentle reminder that He is patient with me. In my petulance I felt myself bristle internally, feeling that He couldn't understand what it was like to not be perfect.

Then I remembered. Jesus grew up. Jesus was perfect in the sense of never having broken fellowship with the Father. He never sinned. But He was not perfect in that He must have made grammatical or spelling mistakes as He was learning language. He did not suddenly know how to do carpentry. He learned from Joseph, in the workshop, or on the job. He had to learn, and undoubtedly made mistakes. Jesus Christ knows what it is like to not know things and to have to learn them.

This gives me hope. We have a God who knows what it is to learn and to grow. His growth sanctifies my growth. I can give myself the grace to grow and be in process.

Jesus' birth, which we celebrate at Christmas, gives me grace for growth.

....

Questions:

What recent mistake of yours left you feeling frustrated?

What are some areas of growth for you?

Can you give yourself grace for your growth?

9 - THE ADVENT OF MYSTERY

Suggested Reading: John 1: 1-18

Do you like being confused?

I don't. I like to understand things. If I don't understand something, I study, research, and ponder. I pick it apart mentally, and sometimes physically, to try to see what makes it work, to unravel the mystery.

This curiosity and desire to understand is a gift from God. Many of the mysteries of life are like puzzles we are meant to explore and solve. God made us curious and put us into a world full of puzzles and conundrums. It must bring Him joy to watch us puzzling over things and solving problems. I know I enjoy figuring things out.

Some things are beyond us because they are too small and we do not have the tools to see or understand them – like atoms. No one has ever seen an atom, or an electron. We know they exist and we can interact with them, but even with our finest tools, we cannot actually see them. Not yet, but someday we might.

But there are other things that are beyond us, not because they are too small, but because we are. God's thoughts and abilities are so far beyond ours that we will never understand them. There are mysteries that are meant to inspire awe and to remind us that we are small.

These awe-inspiring mysteries cause us to place our hands over our mouths, like Job, and shake our heads in wonder. The incarnation is one of these mysteries.

How can a human body contain the Creator of the universe?! At 93 million miles, we are at a safe distance from the Sun. Any closer and we would be destroyed by the heat and power. But the One who made the Sun, and all the stars that dwarf the Sun, was crammed into the womb of a teenage girl; and yet, she was not destroyed. The baby was born, wearing skin like ours, and this God-man walked among us and lived with us, and we were not consumed.

This is a mind-boggling, dizzying mystery, and the common ordinary story of Christmas.

....

Questions:

What aspects of God or His character confuse or perplex you?

How can you celebrate the awesome mystery of Christ today?

10 - THE ADVENT OF RIGHTEOUSNESS

Suggested Reading: 2 Corinthians 5:16-21

G.K. Chesterton was invited to enter a writing contest, which posed a single question: What is wrong with the world? His answer was simply, "I am."

Chesterton's witty and succinct answer summarizes an important truth. Man is not righteous.

When we look at the problems of the world, we are tempted to blame others. We might point to the criminal elements of society. Or, we might point to the unrighteous systems put in place by the powers that be (political, economic, religious, or criminal). These are indeed problematic, but there is a deeper problem that is behind all of these problems.

The problem is us. We are not righteous. Our thoughts and desires are not as they should be. There was a time when man and woman lived in perfect harmony with each other and with God. There were unbroken relationships and pure desires, but we mucked it up.

The first man and the first woman chose not to trust God, but to try to make their own way in the world, apart from God. In doing so, they broke the world, they broke their relationship with God, and they broke something inside themselves. We, their children, have been living with the consequences of their choice ever since. We have inherited their warped morality and tendency to desire the wrong things. Theologians call this 'original sin'.

We are all born bearing a bent image of God, and a defect of soul that predisposes us to make unrighteous choices. We are, at our core, unrighteous. This is particularly bad news, because only the lives of righteous people can be deeply intertwined in a loving relationship with a righteous God. So, we need a saviour. We need someone to make us righteous.

Jesus, the baby born that first Christmas, was the first human since the first humans that was born without that bent. He lived a perfect, righteous life, and even while being victimized and executed He did not retaliate in sin. So, God took all the sin of the world, including yours and mine, and placed it on Jesus at His death. In doing so, God reconciled us to Himself. He made Him who knew no sin to become sin so that we might have the bent places in our life straightened out, the unrighteous places removed and replaced with the right-ness of faith and relationship with God.

....

Questions:

What are some areas in your life where you see your unrighteous bent play out?

How can you express your gratitude for God, for His gift of righteousness?

11 - THE ADVENT OF REST

Suggested Reading: Matthew 11: 27-29

Our world is so busy.

There is so much we feel we need to do, and if you ever do get a chance to just sit down and flip on the television or open the computer, you are immediately inundated with more noise and information to fill your mind – not to mention the advertisements that are designed to make you discontent so they can sell you the solution to the problem they have created for you.

Into the midst of this maelstrom of dissatisfaction and activity comes the onset of Christmas and the holiday season. Just when you thought it couldn't get any busier, there is a new round of expectations and activities!

But there is another way.

The Advent season is an invitation to rest. Jesus invited all who were tired and carrying heavy burdens to come to Him and find rest, rest for your soul.

This rest is not the end of all activity. In fact, this invitation to rest is actually an invitation to step into work alongside Jesus. He uses the image of an ox being tied up next to another ox to pull a wagon or a plough as the invitation to rest. This doesn't immediately strike me as restful!

Jesus invites us to learn from Him, because He is gentle and humble. The invitation is to learn to live from a place of trust, to learn to live as Jesus lived.

As we read the story of the life of Jesus on earth, we don't find a man who was lazy or unengaged. Jesus was active and constantly on the move, but He was not busy or harried. He knew that His Father was working everything out. Even the timing of Jesus' birth was precise and according to plan, although I doubt that Mary and Joseph experienced it as such!

Jesus knew that everything was under the control of His loving Father. He often withdrew to quiet places and prayed. He stayed in tune with the Father and therefore was able to be at rest even in the midst of activity.

He offers this same rest to us.

....

Questions:

How does God's offer of rest sound to you?

What burdens can you lay down today?

What can you let Jesus carry for you?

12 - THE ADVENT OF LIGHT

Suggested Reading: John 8:12

When I was a child, I was afraid of the dark. It wasn't something that impacted me every day, but I remember a few times when I was just terrified.

One of my chores was to take out the trash. Once a week, I would gather the trash from the house, take it to the barrels outside, and then drag the barrels from the side of the house to the curb for collection. I have a tendency to put off chores I don't like to do, and one day I put off taking out the trash and forgot about it. Just before bedtime, my mother reminded me and I had to go outside, in the dark, to do my job.

I still remember peering outside into the dark night, afraid to step out onto the porch, let alone beyond the feeble glow of the porch light. There seemed to be so much darkness and so little light. I managed to do the chore that night and make it back into the house unscathed, but I still remember running as if my life depended on it, sure that a claw or talon was going to snag me from behind before I could reach the safety of the well-lit house.

The same work held no terror for me during the day; only at night did it become a frightening proposition. My inability to see in the dark, to not know what was around me, made it scary.

This world is a dark and scary place at times. We do not know what waits for us around the corner of our lives. There are real dangers and reasons to be fearful. There is evil in the world and in the hearts of men. If we were alone in this darkness it would be prudent to be afraid.

But, Jesus is the light of the world. His birth was written in the light of the stars. His life, death, and resurrection lit up and forever changed the universe. Since He Himself is radiance and light, even the darkness is as noonday to Him. He knows all things and understands all things. He is for us! He will never leave us or forsake us.

In His light, we see light. His light shines around us and even shines out from within us. While Jesus was here, He was the light of the world, but now Jesus says that WE are the light of the world, we are children of light. We are His brothers and sisters! We get to live in His light and to shine His light into a world that is dark and afraid and so in need of light.

....

Questions:

What does it mean for you to live in His light?

How can you shine Jesus' light into the world today?

13 - THE ADVENT OF LOVE

Suggested Reading: John 3:16-21

There is a popular misconception about God that seeps into conversations about Him, even among believers. It is the idea that God is different in the Old Testament and the New Testament, almost as if there were two different God's in the Bible: the violent, angry God of plagues and conquest, and the humble, gentle God of healings and sacrificial love.

The story of Christmas is a love story that bridges the two Testaments and demonstrates the unity of Scripture. Perhaps no single Scripture illustrates this better than Jesus' conversation with Nicodemus.

Nicodemus, a Pharisee and member of the ruling council of the Jews, came to Jesus representing himself and others who recognized God's authority in Jesus, but still had some questions. He was one of the foremost teachers in Israel and knew the Scriptures as well as anyone of his day. The Bible he read was our Old Testament, as the New Testament had not yet been written. In a sense, Jesus is explaining New Testament truths to an Old Testament scholar.

It is in this context that Jesus explains the necessity for the Father to send the Son. God gave His one and only Son because He loved the world so much. Jesus is surprised that this Old Testament scholar doesn't understand these things already.

God's Father-heart toward His children is filled with a fierce love. His love will go to amazing ends to keep His people safe, His message pure, and His purposes on track. His fierce love will brook no opposition and is often shown in power in the Old Testament. But this same fierce and compelling Father-heart is demonstrated in the New Testament by His willingness to humble Himself and endure suffering and pain on behalf of His children. It was the same divine love, expressed in different ways.

We desperately need help! We need a Saviour who will rescue us from the World, from the Devil, and from our own wayward hearts. God's love will conquer all opposition... even the opposition that comes from within us.

"God showed how much he loved us by sending his one and only Son into the world so that we might have eternal life through him. This is real love—not that we loved God, but that he loved us and sent his Son as a sacrifice to take away our sins." (1 John 4:9-10)

....

Questions:

In what ways have you sensed or seen God's love for you recently?

How have you been resisting God's love? How can you live as one loved today?

14 - THE ADVENT OF JOY

Suggested Reading: Luke 1:39-55

Aesop told a story about a fox and a lion. The first time the fox saw the lion, he ran away and hid. The second time he saw him, he sat quietly as the lion walked by. The third time, he walked right up to the lion and chatted with him. As the fox became familiar with the lion, his awe and fear he felt at first gradually evaporated. The moral of Aesop's story is familiarity breeds contempt.

I have lived in several countries and have sometimes had the privilege to be the first one to share the message of Christ and Christmas with someone who has never heard the story before. You should see the looks on their faces! It really is a shocking and incredible story. God became man? God was born from the womb of a woman? This is impossible to understand and very difficult to believe.

But for many of my Muslim friends, the most amazing part of the story was that God loved us and reached out to us at all. Add to that, the incredible truth that through the miracles of the incarnation, death, and resurrection of the Christ, the barrier between us and God has been removed, and you have set the stage for an explosion of joy.

The incarnation filled heaven with joy! The baby John leapt in Elizabeth's womb. The angel armies broke into song. The first humans to meet Jesus couldn't contain themselves. The shepherds told everyone they met about the baby. Simeon and Anna couldn't contain their joy in meeting the 8 day old baby messiah in the temple. The wise men told everyone about their search, and they hadn't even met him yet.

Joy unspeakable! Rejoice in the Lord always!

There is a danger for us today. This story is no longer new. The idea that we can approach the holy and powerful King of the Universe is no longer a new or terrifying idea. The miracle of Christmas has become blasé; old news to us.

God is for us and God is with us! While this news is over two-thousand years old, it is still earth-shattering, mind-blowing, soul-stirring good news!

Let's recover the joy this Christmas. Joy to the world indeed!

....

Questions:

What can you do to remind yourself about the joyous news of Christmas?

Is there someone in your life who needs to hear this joyous news?

15 - THE ADVENT OF PEACE

Suggested Reading: Isaiah 9:1-7

Peace is so elusive.

Most people want it, but they don't know how to get it. The world promises peace, but rarely delivers.

Peace as an ideal or a feeling is admirable, but fleeting and hard to pin down. Just when you think you have it, it slips through your fingers and disappears. Political peace is difficult to achieve and precarious, easily upset by the vagaries of circumstance or the emotions of individuals.

God offers peace, but not as the world offers it: not as an abstract ideal, a political compromise, or even as a subjective experience. God offers peace grounded in a person. Jesus is the Prince of Peace.

When the angels announced the birth of the Messiah to the lonely shepherds on the hills outside of Bethlehem, they announced peace on earth and goodwill to men.

Men expected the Messiah to bring peace to their world, but they thought it would be peace through superior firepower. They expected a political Messiah who would bring them military victory over their oppressors, their enemies.

What they did not anticipate was that the Messiah Himself would be peace. Jesus Christ is the embodiment of peace between God and man because

He is God and man. Ever since the Garden of Eden, man and God had been divided, separated from the time when man rejected God and chose to seek knowledge and satisfaction apart from Him.

True peace is grounded in peace with God. The fundamental source of tension and division does not come from outside of us, but is the rupture of relationship between each of us and our Creator. We were created to be with Him, to live in perfect, unbroken relationship with Him and each other, but you and I have yet to experience that in full.

When Jesus was born, peace was born. He demonstrated a life of perfect peace. He was despised and rejected, a man of sorrows and acquainted with grief. He was angry at times, and suffered greatly, but never lost His connection with the Father. In His death, He made a way for us to boldly approach the throne of grace. In His resurrection, He killed death and showed us the power of the peace that is coming when death and separation are forever dead. In His ascension, He sent us the Spirit of peace; the Spirit that causes love, and joy, and peace to flow from within us.

Through the Spirit we are the peacemakers, the children of God, carrying on the work of our Lord and Brother, Jesus. We receive comfort and peace from the Spirit and we become conduits of this peace and ambassadors of reconciliation. Through us, God preaches the Good News of the Prince of Peace born that first Christmas.

....

Questions:

Are you living in a broken relationship with God? With others?

How can you respond to Jesus, the Prince of Peace today?

How can you be an agent of His peace today?

16 - THE ADVENT OF PATIENCE

Suggested Reading: Galatians 4:4-6

Are you naturally patient? I'm not, and as I look around, I don't see a lot of patience in the world these days. In fact, it seems like we are progressively programmed to be less patient, to expect and demand instant everything: information, service, and gratification. We are no longer required to be patient, nor do we desire it.

God refuses to be rushed or bullied. He is not slow as some reckon slowness. He does everything on His perfect timescale. He is the Alpha and the Omega, the beginning and the end of all things. He knows the end from the beginning and He is working all things together for our good, and the good of the world. He is never late, never early, always gets the timing just right.

However, I don't understand His timing. His thoughts are higher than mine; His ways are higher than mine. I do not and cannot understand all the factors at work.

I remember pondering this as I walking down the beach here in Wales, noticing the action of the waves. The tide was going out, so the waves were not crashing, but instead gently rolling up and down between the rocks and over the sand. I noticed that the rocks were well worn; some had taken on impossible shapes beneath the steady motion of the waves. I saw the sand being pushed up and down the beach by the surf. I saw small pebbles rolling around beneath the water, on their way to becoming sand themselves.

As I walked down the beach that day, my mind wandered and I found myself mentally designing a sand making machine, as if the only purpose of the waves was the slow manufacture of sand. I was sure I could design a more efficient system to achieve the same end. As heirs to the industrial and information revolutions, we naturally set out to design and build systems that will efficiently and effectively produce the results that we need, but God's way of doing thing is different and better. It may look inefficient, but we do not see the whole picture.

God is moving and His Kingdom is coming, but all in His own mysterious time and paradoxical ways. I feel such urgency, an impatience for God to move! I want to see all the people healed and the slaves set free. I want to see evil eradicated (both in me and in the world). I want His Kingdom to come and His will to be done NOW!

But God, who knows all things, is patient. He gives me His Spirit of patience. He asks me to trust and to wait upon Him. He promises that when I do, I will soar like an eagle.

At just the right time, God sent His Son. God is not slow as some reckon slowness, but in the fullness of time He came, and He will come again.

....

Questions:

In what ways are you impatient?

What things are you waiting for in life?

Are you content with God's timing?

17 - THE ADVENT OF KINDNESS

Suggested Reading: Psalm 145

My family and I enjoy the movie Evan Almighty. It is a wonderful retelling of the story of Noah, set in modern times. One of the key themes of the film is that the world is changed by one act of random kindness at a time.

You don't hear a lot about kindness these days. It rarely makes the news. But kindness is one of the most powerful things in the world. Kindness changes the world because it changes our hearts and our lives. It is God's kindness that leads us to repentance, and repentance is a change of heart. When hearts change, people change; when people change, cultures change:;when cultures change, the world changes.

God is kind. There is a special word in Hebrew that expresses God's unconditional loving kindness: Hesed. This one term summarizes the tender heart of God toward all that He has made. God is not just loving and kind toward those who love Him. He is loving and kind toward all! I'm so glad, because none of us would have come to Him in the first place had He not been patient and kind in providing for us and drawing us to Himself while we were still resisting Him.

The birth of Christ was a special kindness, a gift to a world which was not expecting it. God did all the work, all the sacrifice, all the reconciling while the world just went about its business.

There is meekness and a willingness to go unrecognized that accompanies true kindness. It's not keeping score and making sure that people are grateful; it flows from a generosity of heart that wants to bless others. God sent His Son into the world, knowing that the world would not welcome Him, would mock and reject Him, and would eventually kill Him. But God gave us His most precious Son anyway.

God's kindness came to us at Christmas, and now we can give that gift to others. His kindness expressed through His people is still leading people to repentance today.

....

Questions:

How has God's kindness changed you? Your heart? To whom can you show kindness today?

18 - THE ADVENT OF GOODNESS

Suggested Reading: Ephesians 5:8-9

Goodness, like kindness, is an underrated virtue. In fact, today it is often used as a negative term, as in "goody two shoes." To be good is to be perceived as weak or naive. To be worldly, jaded, cynical, and tough are attributes of our heroes these days. From Iron Man to Wolverine, our modern heroes may be powerful, but they are unpredictable, deeply flawed, and often not even good. They may have some light in them, but they seem to be mostly shadow. Perhaps this is a result of the pervasive cynicism we confuse with wisdom.

Jesus stands out in the midst of our culture as the ultimate hero, and one that is nothing but good. His motivations and His actions might be puzzling, but that they are good, there is no question. Jesus stands alone with omnipotent power partnered with untainted goodness. His love is unending, His sacrifices immeasurable, and His kindness transforming.

He faced a crowd armed with stones, ready to kill, using just a few words and some scribbling in the sand, and in so doing saved a woman in need. When faced with systematic wickedness and the desecration of a house of prayer for all peoples, Jesus cobbled together a whip from some rope, flipped the tables, and drove the robbers from the temple. He healed the sick, gave sight to the blind, raised the dead, and went about doing good wherever He went. When asked by His Father to lay down His life for the world, He wrestled in prayer, and freely chose to give His life for all of us. He was brave, powerful, and always good.

You would think that His goodness would draw people to Him. But being good is a prophetic act, and those who love the darkness hate the light. Jesus' goodness in the midst of a wicked and depraved world shone brightly and was a challenge to those entrenched darkness. Simple goodness was a threat.

The religious and political leaders of the day were so invested in their own power and prestige that they could not allow someone to wander around doing good. One of the final turning points in the gospel story, the point of no return, was when Jesus brought Lazarus back to life. Jesus loved Lazarus and his sisters, Mary and Martha. He raised Lazarus from the dead as a demonstration of God's power and goodness. The people marvelled! The religious leaders decided to kill him. They all recognized His miracles, but some believed while others plotted murder.

The baby in a manger brought God's goodness into the world, and through us it shines on today. We are the people of light. The Spirit of Christ, of goodness, lives in us.

....

Questions:

What qualities of goodness have you seen in others?

How can you live out of His goodness and shine Jesus' light into the world today?

19 - THE ADVENT OF FAITHFULNESS

Suggested Reading: Luke 2:25-36

What must it have been like to be waiting for the Messiah?

Isaiah's Messianic prophecies were nearly 700 years old, and David's and Moses' prophetic words were much older when Jesus was born. Entire generations lived and died without seeing the promises fulfilled. They must have wondered. They must have questioned. They must have doubted. I find myself looking for fresh signs of God's faithfulness daily; what must it have been like for followers of God to go through their whole lives waiting and longing for what we now have?

In the midst of our struggles and doubts, God remains faithful. I am not as young as I used to be, and as I look back over the years I can trace the fingerprints of the faithful Master in the grooves of my life. I can see that He was working things together for my good, even in times of trial and suffering. My testimony is but a short shadow of the bright radiance of the glory of God's faithfulness revealed through the incarnation.

From the very beginning, as soon as Grandpa Adam and Grandma Eve fell in the Garden of Eden,

God promised to deliver us. He promised that one of our own, a human, would vanquish evil. Through the centuries and the ministry of many prophets He layered promise on promise, telling us more about what this coming saviour would look like and what he would do. He told us about the conquering of evil and the suffering servant. He told us where he would be born, and how he would die.

Generations of His people watched and waited, studying the already ancient texts and looking for their fulfilment. They must have been tempted to despair as they were sent into exile, or when they were oppressed yet again. They must have wondered why God wasn't speaking, or why He seemed entirely absent; all the while they were waiting for Immanuel, God with us.

Then, suddenly there is a star in the sky and a rumour on the wind. Could it be that the Christ, the Messiah of God is Jesus, the son of Joseph and Mary?!

God is always faithful. He always does what He says He will do. His timing is not always what we would desire, but it is always good...it is always perfect. He promised to send His Son and He did. He promised to be with us and to never forsake us. He is always present in and with us by His Spirit. He promised to sustain us until the end, when He will come again, and He will.

......

Questions:
In what ways has God shown His faithfulness to you?
How is God asking you to live out faithfulness today?
How can you rest in God's faithfulness?

20 - THE ADVENT OF GENTLENESS

Suggested Reading: Isaiah 42:1-4

The tenderness and gentleness of God are on display in the story of Advent.

There was no trumpet of royal fanfare as the angel quietly slipped into the presence of Mary and gently told her she had been chosen to be the mother of the Messiah. The news was troubling, but softly delivered.

Joseph, a good and honourable man, planned to gently and quietly break off his engagement to Mary, until his sleep was disturbed by a messenger from heaven. Another angelic visitation, quietly reassuring him that Mary's honour was intact, inviting Joseph to be the adoptive father of the unborn Messiah.

Mary and Joseph shared an uneventful trip to Bethlehem, and when Jesus finally appears from Mary's womb, God's gentleness continues. The King of kings and Lord of lords, the master of powers beyond belief comes to us. He comes to us as a weak and vulnerable baby. What could be gentler than a new-born baby? The holy family lead a quiet, simple life. Neither boldness nor brashness marks this carpenter family. There was nothing about them that attracted special attention as they lived up in the hills, far from the centre of things in Rome or even Jerusalem.

God is patient, kind, and gentle through the story and throughout history.

The King of the Universe is just and powerful. He has structured both the physical and spiritual universe around immutable laws. We have broken the law and we should bear the full consequences and be sentenced for our crimes. But God does not treat us as we deserve. He is patient with His traitorous children. He waits patiently and gently woos us back to Himself. He made a way for justice to be carried out and mercy and gentleness to be carried out as well. He devised a way to take our sins upon Himself. He took the sentence for our crimes and was punished for our wrong choices.

Then, having removed the barrier between us, He quietly and gently slips into our hearts and lives. Through His Holy Spirit the gentle God births His gentleness in us.

.....

Questions:

How does God's gentle love touch your heart?

How can you reflect the gentleness of God in your relationships today?

21 - THE ADVENT OF ABUNDANCE

Suggested Reading: John 10:1-18

In my travels, I have seen extreme poverty. I have seen people trapped, without hope of escape from the downward cycle of scarcity. It is such a horrible thing to witness, let alone experience. I don't know anyone who would knowingly choose poverty, if abundance was available. But I have seen many choose to live spiritually impoverished lives, often in the midst of physical abundance.

It seems that Jesus was getting at this bizarre dichotomy when He spoke about how hard it is for the rich to enter the Kingdom of Heaven. When we are physically comfortable, we tend toward pride and self-satisfaction, the subtle sins that so easily entangle. We somehow begin to feel that we deserve our abundance and we use our wealth to find new diversions, to mask the pain of our spiritual poverty.

Blaise Pascal, the scientist, mathematician, and philosopher, suggested that there is a God shaped hole in the heart of every man. This hole is like a vacuum that demands to be filled. Thirteen hundred years earlier Augustine described the same phenomenon when he observed that our hearts are restless until we find our rest in God. Both men were describing the longing of every human heart for a full heart and a full life.

The baby Jesus was born to bring us abundant life, a full life that flows from a full heart. He promised that anyone who came to Him would be filled to overflowing with the very presence of God; streams of living water welling up and flowing out so we might never thirst again. Imagine living in a desert land and hearing that kind of promise! It sounds too good to be true.

Nothing about God is too good to be true. He is the way, the truth and the life. Through Him, and only through Him, we can come to the Father. With this foundational divine relationship in place, all of life takes on a different tone. We can enjoy all the wonderful things God has given us, when we are not trying to draw from them more than they can supply.

The abundant life is not necessarily a life of abundance. It is a life of contentment whatever the circumstances, because you know the One who works all circumstances together for your good. It is the life Christ lived, and is now available to us in Him and because of Him.

....

Questions:

What is preventing you from experiencing the abundant life?

Is there something with which you have been trying to fill your heart?

How can you seek the abundant life in and through Jesus?

22 - THE ADVENT OF SELF-CONTROL

Suggested Reading: 2 Peter 1:3-6

Choices.

There is a saying that life is what happens while you are making other plans. This pithy maxim hints at the fact that our lives are largely made up of a myriad of small choices. These choices determine the overall direction of our lives. It is not our intentions that determine our direction, but the actual choices that we make and the consequences that follow those choices.

Mary was chosen, but she had a choice. She chose to submit to the will of God as revealed through the angel Gabriel. It is difficult for us to imagine the path before the unwed Galilean peasant girl. In her initial response to the angel, she was confused and disturbed. She knew that to be found pregnant without a husband might well mean her death. She questioned the angel, but at the end of the conversation, she chose to trust and pledged herself to God's service.

Joseph too had a choice. He must have been very upset when he found that his bride to be was pregnant. He had decided not to press charges, which would have meant her death and that of the unborn child. He was not about to marry her under the circumstances, until he too had an angelic visitor who reminded him of the ancient prophecies. He chose to believe the angel and cherished Mary and her unborn child.

Without the choices of these two nobodies, simple people from a small town, the Messiah would not have been born. Imagine the pressure they would have felt to make the opposite choices. Imagine the fear and the uncertainty. From where we sit, two thousand years later, reading the familiar story, we can miss the stress and difficulty, and in doing so we miss the beauty of their self-control. They exercised their will and became a part of the greatest story ever lived.

As Jesus grew in wisdom and in stature, in favour with God and man, He learned obedience through suffering. What must it have been like for Him to suffer the slings and arrows of outrageous treatment at the hands of sinful man, when the power of heaven was His to command? He wrestled in the Garden of Gethsemane, facing a torturous death, but chose to endure the pain and shame of the cross in obedience to the will of the Father. Through His death and resurrection, He made a way for us to live with God, and His self-control can become ours.

We have daily choices and wrestle with conflicting desires. In this we are not alone, we have the Spirit of Christ in us, the Spirit of self-control to show us the way and help us to choose it.

...

Questions:
What choices do you have before you today?
What might God be asking you to do?
What areas of your life require self-control today?

23 - THE ADVENT OF LIFE

Suggested Reading: John 17:1-5

Life is more than our heartbeat and our brainwaves. Life is more than just continuing to breathe and think and move. Real life is more than just existing. All people exist but not all people truly live.

Many of us settle for mere existence. Our culture teaches us that life is what we own. It tells us that he who dies with the most toys wins. The reality is that he who dies with the most toys still dies, and his toys are useless to him. But there is another way, a way to live and never die.

Jesus defined real life, the eternal kind of life, as knowing God. The moment we come to know God, we become spiritually alive; we receive the Holy Spirit, and become partakers of the divine nature. When this happens, we have embarked on the journey of becoming who we really are. We begin to live out our mandate to be the image of God, little representatives of Christ, each expressing our individual gifts and unique facets of the glory of God. Our core comes alive, and we become ever more ourselves as we learn to live and never die, to live the eternal kind of life.

When the baby Jesus breathed His first earthly breath, life came to live among us. Jesus Himself was and is the way, the truth, and the life. He is life made visible to us. He is the source and essence of life. He lived life to the full, showing us what the abundant and full life can look like. It wasn't a life of material riches, but it was a rich life. He walked our dusty roads, breathed our air, and ate our food. He worked and paid taxes and lived a fully human life, a life fully alive.

He is our model, our older brother, the firstborn in our family. Through His life, death, and resurrection, He made a way for us to follow in His footsteps. We can know God and have real life. Through His life we find life.

Life was born at Christmas.

Questions:

Have you entered into the eternal kind of life with Jesus?

How can you nurture this life?

How can you get to know Jesus better today?

24 - THE ADVENT OF RELATIONSHIP

Suggested Reading: 1 John 1 and 1 John 5:11-12

God designed and created us as relational beings; at our core we are relational. In the Garden of Eden, humanity and divinity were in perfect fellowship – no division, no confusion, no distance, perfect unbroken relationship. This is what we were made for. Our hearts long for it, our bodies were made for it, our minds were created for this end.

But we lost it. Like a vase shattered beyond repair, we broke relationship and this broke the world. But the divine potter was on the case. He had a plan and was working His plan out through the ages, to remake the world, to make all things new.

At just the right time, He sent His Son into the world not to condemn the world but to save the world through Him.

The birth of Christ was the dawning of a new age in humanity's relationship with God. In Christ, God and man were together again, in unbroken and perfect relationship. As He lived and grew and learned, Jesus lived the perfect life, a human life in perfect unity with the Father. He always did exactly what the Father wanted and lived in perfect trust in the Father. It was not without struggle, as we see in the Garden of Gethsemane, but it was a life of perfect obedience – a full life, an abundant life, a relational life.

In Christ, the God who was with us in Spirit was now one of us. God always saw and understood us, but in Jesus Christ, we can see and understand God in new ways. We hear His voice and see His actions lived out on our plane of existence. So, the life of Christ is both a perfect human life model for us, and a demonstration of the Divine to us. He left the Spirit with us, so that even now, although we see through a glass darkly, He lives in us. We know He is always with us and will never forsake us.

We look back on the coming of Christ with awe and affection, and we look forward to the coming of Christ with hope and expectation. From the Garden of Eden, through the Garden of Gethsemane, to the garden of God in the new heaven and new earth, it has always been about relationship.

We were designed for relationship with God. As it was in the beginning, so it will always be. Christ in us the hope of glory.

Questions:
In what ways are you intentionally cultivating and enjoying your relationship with God?
How does your relationship with God change you and your relationships with others?

BENEDICTION

May your gifts this Christmas remind you of the gift of Christ. May your generosity remind you of the generosity of the Father. May your relationships with others remind you of the fellowship of the Spirit. May you know the joy of the angels, the eagerness of the shepherds and the peace of the Christ child. May the blessing of God almighty, the Father, the Son, and the Holy Spirit, be among you and remain with you always; and may you and yours have a very Merry Christmas.

(Adapted from a Church of England Advent blessing)

ABOUT THE AUTHOR

Thaddaeus Joseph MacLeslie has been involved in a variety Christian ministries since 1990, including pastoring, church planting, leadership development, prayer, and spiritual formation.

He currently lives in the UK with his wife and two children where he leads a team focused on prayer and spiritual formation. You'll often find him walking the fields with his dog, reading a book, or enjoying a warm cup of coffee.

Other books by T.J. MacLeslie:

Pursuit of a Thirsty Fool
For more information, please visit www.thirstyfool.com

Designed for Relationship
For more information, please visit www.dfrbook.com

Connect online:
Twitter – @TJMacLeslie
Website – www.about.me/tj_macleslie
Email: TJMacLeslie@gmail.com

58280926R00041

Made in the USA
San Bernardino, CA
26 November 2017